The Life and Legacy of Robin Windsor:

From Strictly to Stardom, the Inspirational Story of a Dance Icon

LEGACY HISTORY

All rights reserved. No part of this publication may be reproduced, distributed, or transmitted in any form or by any means, including photocopying, recording, or other electronic or mechanical methods, without the prior written permission of the publisher, except in the case of brief quotations embodied in critical reviews and certain other noncommercial uses permitted by copyright law.

© **LEGACY HISTORY, 2024.**

TABLE OF CONTENTS

TABLE OF CONTENTS	1
Introduction:	4
Welcome to the World of Robin Windsor	4
A Brief Overview of His Career and Legacy	5
Chapter 1:	9
Early Life and Beginnings	9
Childhood and Family Background	9
Discovering a Passion for Dance	10
Early Training and Influences	12
Chapter 2:	14
The Road to Stardom	14
Joining the Competitive Dance Circuit	14
Breaking into the Entertainment Industry	16
Rise to Prominence in the Dance World	17
Chapter 3:	21
Strictly Come Dancing Journey	21
Joining the Cast of Strictly Come Dancing	21
Memorable Partnerships and Performances	22
Highlights, Challenges, and Behind-the-Scenes Insights	24
Chapter 4:	26
Life Beyond Strictly	26
Post-Strictly Career Ventures	26

Stage Shows, Tours, and Other Projects	28
Expanding His Influence and Reach	30

Chapter 5: 33

Personal Life and Relationships 33

    Insights into Robin's Personal Life 34

    Close Relationships, Friendships, and Family 35

Chapter 6: 38

Facing Adversity and Overcoming Challenges 38

    Coping with Setbacks and Obstacles 39

    Dealing with Injuries and Personal Struggles 40

    Resilience and Triumph in the Face of Adversity 42

Chapter 7: 44

Impact and Legacy 44

    Contributions to Charity and Philanthropy 44

    Remembering Robin: Tributes and Remembrances 46

Conclusion 48

    His Enduring Legacy and Continued Inspiration 48

Introduction:

Welcome to the World of Robin Windsor

Step into the vibrant world of dance, where passion, talent, and dedication converge to create magic on the dance floor. In this captivating journey, we invite you to discover the life and legacy of one of ballroom dancing's most beloved figures: Robin Windsor. With his infectious energy, mesmerizing performances, and unwavering commitment to his craft, Robin enchanted audiences around the world and left an indelible mark on the dance community.

A Brief Overview of His Career and Legacy

Robin Windsor's journey into the world of dance began with a spark of passion ignited in his childhood. Born and raised in the United Kingdom, Robin discovered his love for dance at a young age, drawn to the grace, rhythm, and expression it offered. Fuelled by determination and a relentless pursuit of excellence, he embarked on a journey that would see him rise to prominence as one of the most accomplished dancers of his generation.

Robin's career reached new heights when he joined the cast of the iconic BBC television series, Strictly Come Dancing. With his impeccable technique, charismatic stage presence, and undeniable charm, Robin quickly became a fan favorite on the show. Partnering with celebrities such as Deborah Meaden, Lisa Riley, Anita Dobson, and Patsy Kensit, he dazzled audiences with his electrifying performances and unforgettable routines.

Beyond his success on Strictly Come Dancing, Robin's influence extended far beyond the confines of the ballroom. He was a trailblazer in the world of competitive dance, earning accolades and recognition for his unparalleled skill and artistry. Whether performing on stage, teaching aspiring dancers, or sharing his passion for dance with the world, Robin's impact was profound and far-reaching.

Throughout his illustrious career, Robin remained true to his roots, never losing sight of the joy and passion that first drew him to dance. His commitment to excellence, coupled with his infectious enthusiasm and genuine love for his art, endeared him to fans and colleagues alike. He was not only a gifted dancer but also a beloved mentor, friend, and inspiration to all who had the privilege of knowing him.

His legacy lives on in the hearts of those who were touched by his talent and generosity of spirit, and his influence continues to shape the world of dance for generations to come.

Come, celebrate the life, artistry, and enduring legacy of Robin Windsor—a true icon of the dance world. Welcome to a world of passion, rhythm, and boundless creativity. Welcome to the world of Robin Windsor.

Chapter 1:

Early Life and Beginnings

In the small town of Grimsby, nestled along the eastern coast of England, a young boy named Robin Windsor embarked on a journey that would ignite his passion for dance and shape the course of his life. Born into a loving family with a deep appreciation for the arts, Robin's early years were filled with laughter, music, and a sense of wonder.

Childhood and Family Background

Robin Windsor was born on September 15, 1979, in Ipswich, Suffolk, England. Raised in a close-knit household, Robin was the youngest of three siblings, surrounded by the love and support of his parents and extended family. His upbringing was infused with creativity, as his parents fostered an environment where imagination was encouraged and artistic expression was celebrated. From an early age, Robin was exposed to the world of performance, attending local theater productions and dance recitals with his family.

Discovering a Passion for Dance

It was during one of these outings that Robin's fascination with dance was sparked. Mesmerized by the grace and beauty of the performers on stage, he felt a stirring within him—a longing to move, to express himself through movement in a way that words could not. From that moment on, dance became Robin's truest form of self-expression, a language through which he could communicate his deepest emotions and aspirations.

As he grew older, Robin's passion for dance only intensified. He spent countless hours practicing in front of the mirror, choreographing routines in his bedroom, and immersing himself in the world of dance through books, videos, and classes. Despite the challenges and uncertainties that lay ahead, Robin remained steadfast in his pursuit of his dreams, fueled by a burning desire to share his love of dance with the world.

Early Training and Influences

Determined to hone his craft and refine his skills, Robin sought out formal training from some of the most respected instructors in the industry. Under their guidance, he immersed himself in the technical intricacies of ballet, jazz, and contemporary dance, mastering the fundamentals and laying the groundwork for his future success.

As he delved deeper into the world of dance, Robin found inspiration in the performances of legendary dancers and choreographers who had come before him. From Fred Astaire and Gene Kelly to Mikhail Baryshnikov and Bob Fosse, each artist left an indelible mark on Robin's artistic sensibility, shaping his approach to movement and performance in profound ways.

Chapter 2:

The Road to Stardom

Joining the Competitive Dance Circuit

As a young dancer with dreams of making it big, Robin Windsor embarked on a journey that would take him from local dance studios to the grand stages of the world. Eager to test his skills and push himself to new heights, he made his foray into the competitive dance circuit with unwavering determination and a hunger for success.

From regional competitions to national championships, Robin honed his craft on the dance floor, dazzling judges and audiences alike with his precision, passion, and undeniable charisma. With each competition, he gained invaluable experience and insights, refining his technique and sharpening his competitive edge.

It was during these formative years that Robin forged lifelong friendships and mentorships with fellow dancers and coaches who would shape his journey and influence his artistic development. Together, they shared triumphs and setbacks, victories and defeats, supporting each other through the highs and lows of the competitive dance world.

Breaking into the Entertainment Industry

Armed with talent, ambition, and an insatiable appetite for success, Robin set his sights on breaking into the entertainment industry—a daunting challenge for any aspiring dancer. Undeterred by the fierce competition and countless auditions, he seized every opportunity to showcase his skills and prove himself worthy of the spotlight.

With determination as his compass and resilience as his armor, Robin navigated the highs and lows of the entertainment industry with grace and perseverance. From small-scale productions to high-profile events, he embraced each opportunity as a chance to shine, leaving a lasting impression on casting directors, producers, and fellow performers.

It was not long before Robin's star began to rise, as his talent and charisma caught the attention of industry insiders and audiences alike. With each new role and performance, he captivated hearts and minds, earning accolades and recognition for his exceptional talent and versatility as a dancer.

Rise to Prominence in the Dance World

As Robin's reputation grew, so too did his opportunities, propelling him to the forefront of the dance world with remarkable speed and agility. With a string of successes under his belt, he emerged as a rising star—a force to be reckoned with on both stage and screen.

One of the pivotal moments in Robin's career came when he was invited to join the cast of the iconic BBC television series, *Strictly Come Dancing*. Stepping onto the hallowed dance floor of the Strictly ballroom, he embarked on a journey that would catapult him to stardom and cement his status as one of the show's most beloved professional dancers.

Partnering with celebrities such as Deborah Meaden, Lisa Riley, Anita Dobson, and Patsy Kensit, Robin mesmerized audiences with his electrifying performances and flawless technique. With each paso doble, cha-cha, and waltz, he captured the hearts of millions, earning rave reviews and standing ovations from fans and judges alike.

Beyond his success on Strictly Come Dancing, Robin's influence extended far beyond the confines of the ballroom. He became a beacon of inspiration for aspiring dancers around the world, demonstrating the transformative power of dance to uplift, empower, and unite people from all walks of life.

As Robin's star continued to rise, he seized every opportunity to share his passion for dance with the world, whether through stage shows, television appearances, or charitable endeavors. With each step he took, he left an indelible mark on the dance world—a legacy of talent, passion, and unwavering dedication that continues to inspire and uplift dancers and fans around the world.

Chapter 3:

Strictly Come Dancing Journey

Joining the Cast of Strictly Come Dancing

Robin Windsor's journey on *Strictly Come Dancing* began in 2010 when he first graced the illustrious ballroom floor as a professional dancer. His infectious energy, impeccable technique, and undeniable charm quickly endeared him to audiences and made him a fan favorite from the start. Robin's debut season saw him partnered with actress Patsy Kensit, marking the beginning of a memorable tenure on one of the UK's most beloved television shows.

Memorable Partnerships and Performances

Throughout his time on Strictly, Robin formed memorable partnerships with a diverse array of celebrity contestants, each bringing their own unique personalities, strengths, and challenges to the dance floor. From business tycoons to soap opera stars, Robin approached each partnership with enthusiasm, creativity, and a genuine desire to bring out the best in his celebrity counterpart.

One of the highlights of Robin's Strictly journey was his partnership with businesswoman and TV personality Deborah Meaden. Together, they captivated audiences with their dynamic performances, infectious chemistry, and fearless approach to the competition. Their partnership showcased Robin's ability to adapt his choreography to suit his partner's strengths, resulting in memorable routines that left a lasting impression on judges and fans alike.

Another standout partnership was with actress and presenter Lisa Riley. With her boundless energy and infectious personality, Lisa brought a sense of joy and vitality to the dance floor, while Robin provided the skill, guidance, and support she needed to shine. Their partnership was a true testament to the transformative power of dance to bring people together and inspire audiences of all ages.

Highlights, Challenges, and Behind-the-Scenes Insights

Robin's journey on *Strictly Come Dancing* was filled with both highs and lows, triumphs and challenges, moments of joy and moments of frustration. Behind the glitz and glamour of the ballroom, he faced grueling rehearsals, intense competition, and the pressure to deliver flawless performances week after week.

Yet, amid the challenges, there were also moments of sheer exhilaration and triumph. From receiving standing ovations from the judges to earning perfect scores from the notoriously tough panel, Robin experienced the thrill of pushing himself to new heights and exceeding his own expectations as a dancer.

Behind the scenes, From early morning rehearsals to late-night costume fittings, he shared the camaraderie, laughter, and occasional tears that defined life on the set of the show.

He had danced his heart out, forged lifelong friendships, and inspired millions of viewers with his talent, passion, and unwavering dedication to his craft.

Chapter 4:

Life Beyond Strictly

After his exhilarating journey on Strictly Come Dancing, Robin Windsor's life took on new dimensions as he ventured into the world beyond the glittering ballroom. With his talent, charm, and boundless energy, he embarked on a diverse array of career ventures, stage shows, tours, and projects that showcased his versatility as a dancer and entertainer.

Post-Strictly Career Ventures

Transitioning from the high-pressure environment of a televised dance competition to the wide-open landscape of post-Strictly life, Robin wasted no time in exploring new opportunities and avenues for artistic expression, charting his course for the future. His time on Strictly had solidified his reputation as a consummate professional and a crowd favorite, paving the way for exciting new ventures in the world of dance and entertainment.

With a wealth of experience and a legion of fans behind him, he sought out new opportunities to share his passion for dance with audiences around the world. From television appearances to guest performances at prestigious events, Robin's star continued to rise as he carved out a niche for himself in the entertainment industry.

One of the highlights of Robin's post-Strictly career was his involvement in stage productions and live shows. From West End productions to international tours, he dazzled audiences with his electrifying performances and captivating stage presence. Whether starring in musicals, cabaret shows, or dance extravaganzas, Robin brought his trademark flair and charisma to every performance, leaving audiences spellbound and craving more.

Stage Shows, Tours, and Other Projects

As a seasoned performer with a knack for captivating audiences, Robin found himself in high demand for stage shows, tours, and other projects that showcased his talent and versatility as a dancer and entertainer. From headlining his own solo shows to collaborating with other artists and performers, he embraced each opportunity as a chance to push the boundaries of his artistry and connect with audiences on a deeper level.

One of the most memorable projects of Robin's post-Strictly career was his involvement in *Come What May,* a Moulin Rouge tribute show that paid homage to the iconic film and its timeless music. As one of the show's principal dancers and choreographers, Robin brought his unique blend of passion, creativity, and technical skill to the stage, earning rave reviews and standing ovations from audiences around the world.

In addition to his work on stage, Robin also found success in other creative endeavors, including television appearances, commercial endorsements, and charitable initiatives. Whether showcasing his dancing prowess on talk shows and variety programs or lending his support to worthy causes and philanthropic endeavors, he continued to expand his influence and reach, using his platform to inspire and uplift others.

Expanding His Influence and Reach

Beyond the stage and screen, Robin's influence extended far beyond the confines of the entertainment industry. As a beloved figure in the world of dance, he became a role model and mentor for aspiring dancers around the world, offering guidance, encouragement, and support to those who shared his passion for movement and expression.

Through workshops, masterclasses, and educational initiatives, Robin shared his knowledge, expertise, and love of dance with students of all ages and skill levels, inspiring them to pursue their dreams and embrace the transformative power of dance in their own lives. Whether teaching a beginner's class or coaching seasoned professionals, he approached each opportunity with enthusiasm, patience, and a genuine desire to empower others.

As he continued to expand his influence and reach, Robin remained true to his roots, never losing sight of the joy and passion that first drew him to dance. From his electrifying performances on stage to his tireless advocacy for the art of dance, he left an indelible mark on the hearts and minds of all who had the privilege of experiencing his talent, charisma, and boundless energy.

Chapter 5:

Personal Life and Relationships

As much as Robin Windsor dazzled audiences with his captivating performances and infectious energy on the dance floor, there was a private side to the beloved dancer that few were privileged to see.

Getting insights into the man behind the spotlight and the close bonds that shaped his journey.

Insights into Robin's Personal Life

Away from the glitz and glamour of the entertainment industry, Robin cherished the simple pleasures of life and found solace in the quiet moments spent with loved ones. He was a deeply introspective individual, with a keen intellect and a passion for learning and self-discovery. Whether exploring new interests, pursuing creative endeavors, or simply enjoying the beauty of the natural world, Robin found fulfillment in the pursuit of knowledge, growth, and personal development.

Despite the demands of his career, Robin made it a priority to nurture his personal well-being and maintain a healthy work-life balance. He valued the importance of self-care, mindfulness, and mental health, recognizing that true happiness and fulfillment could only be found by honoring one's own needs and aspirations. Through his example, he inspired others to prioritize self-care and make time for the things that truly mattered in life.

Close Relationships, Friendships, and Family

At the heart of Robin's personal life were the close relationships, friendships, and family bonds that sustained him through life's ups and downs. He was a loyal and devoted friend, always there to offer support, encouragement, and a listening ear to those in need. Whether sharing a laugh over a cup of coffee or lending a shoulder to cry on in times of trouble, Robin's presence brought comfort and joy to those around him.

Among his closest friends and confidants were fellow dancers, colleagues, and collaborators who shared his passion for dance and the arts. Together, they formed a tight-knit community bound by a shared love of creativity, expression, and the pursuit of excellence. Through their friendships and collaborations, Robin found strength, inspiration, and camaraderie, forging lifelong connections that enriched his life and career.

But perhaps the most cherished relationships in Robin's life were those with his family—the steadfast pillars of love, support, and guidance that anchored him through life's tumultuous waters. From his parents and siblings to extended family members and loved ones, Robin's family provided a nurturing environment where he could thrive, grow, and pursue his dreams with confidence and courage.

As he navigated the highs and lows of his career, Robin's family stood by his side, offering unwavering love and encouragement every step of the way. Whether cheering him on from the audience at a dance competition or celebrating his successes with pride and joy, they were his constant source of strength and inspiration, reminding him of the importance of love, loyalty, and connection in a world that often seemed chaotic and unpredictable.

Chapter 6:

Facing Adversity and Overcoming Challenges

In the glittering world of dance, where grace and beauty reign supreme, Robin Windsor's journey was not without its share of challenges and setbacks. From his early days on Strictly Come Dancing to his contributions to the dance community and his personal struggles, Robin's resilience and determination were tested time and again.

Coping with Setbacks and Obstacles

Throughout his career, Robin encountered numerous setbacks and obstacles that tested his resolve and pushed him to his limits. From early eliminations on *Strictly Come Dancing* to career-threatening injuries, he faced moments of doubt and uncertainty that threatened to derail his dreams. Yet, with each setback, Robin found the strength and determination to pick himself up, dust himself off, and keep moving forward.

One of the greatest challenges Robin faced was the intense pressure and scrutiny that came with being a professional dancer in the public eye. From harsh critiques to negative feedback, he had to learn to navigate the highs and lows of the entertainment industry with grace and resilience. Through it all, he remained steadfast in his belief in himself and his abilities, refusing to let the opinions of others define his worth or dictate his path.

Dealing with Injuries and Personal Struggles

As a dancer, Robin understood the physical and emotional toll that his art form could exact. From grueling rehearsals to demanding performances, he pushed his body to its limits, often at the expense of his own well-being. Over the years, he experienced his fair share of injuries and setbacks, from sprains and strains to more serious ailments that threatened to sideline him from the stage. Such as the Back surgery he had during Series 12 of *Strictly Come Dancing,*which was as a result of a serious Back Injury, afterwards he quit the show because they won't call him back the next year.

Yet, even in the face of adversity, Robin refused to let his injuries define him or hold him back. With the support of his friends, family, and colleagues, he embarked on a journey of healing and rehabilitation, determined to overcome the physical and emotional challenges that stood in his way. Through perseverance, patience, and a relentless commitment to his craft, Robin emerged from each setback stronger, more resilient, and more determined than ever to pursue his passion for dance.

Resilience and Triumph in the Face of Adversity

Time and time again, he proved himself to be a fighter—a warrior on the dance floor, a beacon of hope and inspiration for all who knew him.

Whether facing career setbacks, personal struggles, or physical challenges, Robin approached each obstacle with courage, grace, and unwavering determination. Through sheer force of will and an unshakeable belief in himself, he transformed adversity into opportunity, turning setbacks into stepping stones on the path to greatness.

As he danced his way through life, Robin Windsor became a symbol of resilience, tenacity, and the indomitable human spirit. His journey serves as a powerful reminder that, no matter the obstacles we face, we have the strength and resilience within us to overcome them and emerge stronger, wiser, and more resilient than ever before.

In the end, it is not the challenges we encounter that define us, but how we choose to face them—with courage, grace, and unwavering determination. And in the case of Robin Windsor, his resilience in the face of adversity serves as a shining example of the power of the human spirit to triumph over even the greatest of obstacles.

Chapter 7:

Impact and Legacy

Robin Windsor's impact on the dance community transcends his performances on *Strictly Come Dancing* and stage shows. His influence, contributions to charity, and the lasting memories he left behind continue to resonate within the hearts of those he touched.

Contributions to Charity and Philanthropy

Beyond his achievements as a dancer and entertainer, Robin was also a passionate advocate for charitable causes and philanthropic endeavors. Throughout his career, he lent his support to numerous charitable organizations, using his platform to raise awareness and funds for causes close to his heart.

Whether participating in charity dance events, hosting fundraising galas, or lending his name to charitable initiatives, Robin remained dedicated to making a positive impact in the lives of others. His generosity, compassion, and commitment to giving back served as an inspiration to all who knew him, reminding us of the importance of using our talents and resources to make a difference in the world.

Remembering Robin: Tributes and Remembrances

Following Robin's untimely passing, tributes and remembrances poured in from friends, colleagues, and fans around the world. From fellow dancers to television personalities, everyone who had the privilege of knowing Robin shared heartfelt stories and fond memories of their time with him.

Strictly Come Dancing co-star James Jordan paid tribute to Robin, remembering him as a caring and fun-loving friend. He spoke of Robin's infectious energy and boundless kindness, recalling the joy he brought to everyone around him. Others, including TV presenter Kirsty Gallacher and

Strictly choreographer Patrick Helm, also expressed their sadness at Robin's passing, remembering him as a beloved figure in the dance community.

As the dance world mourns the loss of one of its brightest stars, Robin Windsor's legacy lives on in the hearts and memories of all who had the privilege of knowing him. His impact on the dance community, his contributions to charity, and the lasting friendships he forged serve as a testament to the power of passion, perseverance, and the indomitable human spirit. Though he may be gone, his spirit will continue to inspire dancers and fans alike for generations to come.

Conclusion

His Enduring Legacy and Continued Inspiration

As we bid farewell to Robin Windsor, we are reminded of the remarkable journey of a man who danced his way into the hearts of millions, we are reminded of the enduring legacy he leaves behind—a legacy of passion, perseverance, and the transformative power of dance.

Throughout his life, Robin embodied the values of hard work, dedication, and humility, earning the respect and admiration of colleagues, fans, and friends alike. His infectious energy, boundless enthusiasm, and genuine love for dance endeared him to audiences around the world, leaving an indelible mark on the hearts and minds of all who had the privilege of knowing him.

Though he may no longer be with us, Robin's spirit lives on in the hearts and memories of all who had the privilege of knowing him, witnessing his talent, his passion, and his enduring spirit.. His enduring legacy serves as a beacon of hope and inspiration for dancers and fans around the world, reminding us of the boundless potential that lies within each of us to make a difference in the world through our talents, our passions, and our unwavering commitment to excellence.

As we celebrate Robin's life and legacy, let us honor his memory by continuing to embrace the joy of dance, the spirit of perseverance, and the belief that anything is possible with dedication, hard work, and a little bit of magic. Robin Windsor may have danced his way into eternity, but his legacy will continue to inspire and uplift us for generations to come.

51

Printed in Great Britain
by Amazon